BLUE CORN TONGUE

Volume 97

Sun Tracks

SERIES EDITOR

Ofelia Zepeda

EDITORIAL COMMITTEE

Larry Evers

Joy Harjo

Geary Hobson

Irvin Morris

Simon J. Ortiz

Craig Santos Perez

Kate Shanley

Leslie Marmon Silko

Luci Tapahonso

PRAISE FOR AMBER MCCRARY

"This collection describes a life woven together through the topography of the land examining elements of language, love, and family. There is a distinct point of view that encompasses the dialectical nature of belonging. Traveling alongside the poet in tender and sometimes funny moments, I found myself wanting to share these poems with friends."

—**Naomi Ortiz**, author of *Rituals for Climate Change*

"McCrary's collection is one that only she could write. It is a mixtape from a thirty-something Diné punk girl with tracks about love and friendship, but also environmental destruction and language loss."

—**Casandra López**, author of *Brother Bullet*

"*Blue Corn Tongue: Poems in the Mouth of the Desert* is a wonder of a book full of 'Weaving words with nostalgic tongues, heirloom futures and circular knowledge.' Multilingual, expansive, and courageously written, these poems are an ecosystem of love and place that moves the reader through a sensory landscape of frank emotion and complex beauty. Lovers 'maized through the rooms' of a boarding school exhibit 'familiar as grandma's tortillas 'in one poem and inhabit a space where 'desert honey pulsates' in another. Both strikingly original and deeply rooted, this book is a marvel to behold."

—**Laura Da'**, author of *Instruments of the True Measure*

"In the middle of the desert, a woman holds a poem. And a river begins to flow. McCray's stunning poems tell the story of the seed, the root, and the inevitable flower. Anchored in the question 'How does language open?' this experimental, brave, and intimate book is a must-read."

—**Margarita Pintado Burgos**, author of *Ojo en Celo / Eye in Heat*

"Equal parts tender and defiant, McCrary's *Blue Corn Tongue* laps up landscape and love alike. Propelled by a moving sensuousness, this collection reframes relations between poet, lover, relatives, and the history binding them. Through striking visuals, rich carnality, and the occasional unexpected laugh, McCrary's work celebrates and challenges what it means to dream and desire from within O'odham Jeweḍ and Dinétah."

—**Oscar Mancinas**, author of *To Live and Die in El Valle*

"Amber McCrary is a poet of generational talent who has written a masterful work of staggering beauty. One cannot help but read and reread *Blue Corn Tongue* with a sense of awe and gratitude for having witnessed, for having been gifted with a poetry that does the important work of documenting and honoring the narratives of her rich culture. I am holding something important in my hands, in this time. I am going to be holding this book close to the heart for years to come because it means that much to me."

—**Truong Tran**, author of *Book of the Other*

"In Amber McCrary's poems, the deserts are rich with sweet honey. This sumptuous debut celebrates Indigenous love, the Navajo language, corn kernels grinding on the tongue—lush life upon life. *Blue Corn Tongue* teaches me to indulge in intimacy, to find it essential, even as it is haunted by loss. I am thankful for this collection, which insists on remaining abundant and unashamed."

—**Erin Marie Lynch**, author of *Removal Acts*

"Between canyons of love and loss and the spines of lost language, Amber's poems emerge from a blue corn dawn with prose that must be taken like a sacrament. Profoundly intimate and raw, McCrary circumvents the assumption that the desert is devoid of life. Rather, it is a sensual place where cacti and desert plants fruit, bloom, and spill their seeds for future generations. McCrary's meditations on language, Diné history, and reservation towns capture the duality of the desert rain, packed with torrential grief or sweet and gentle like Mother Rain. Either way, McCrary's poems are deeply replenishing and as thrilling as a lightening streak."

—**Stacie Shannon Denetsosie**, author of *The Missing Morningstar and Other Stories*

"Filled with stylistically innovative poems that embody place and emerge from 'the mouth of deserts,' *Blue Corn Tongue* carries both 'generational grief' and reclamation. McCrary's poetry claims the Diné language and a vibrant matrilineal power through a 'kin kind of tongue.' These intimate poems are filled with lush, tactile images and populated with beings and beliefs that have survived colonization. Over and over, they celebrate 'something laws cannot govern.'"

—**Kimberly Blaeser**, author of *Ancient Light* and Wisconsin poet laureate, 2015–16

BLUE CORN TONGUE

Poems in the Mouth of the Desert

AMBER MCCRARY

THE UNIVERSITY OF
ARIZONA PRESS

TUCSON

The University of Arizona Press
www.uapress.arizona.edu

We respectfully acknowledge the University of Arizona is on the land and territories of Indigenous peoples. Today, Arizona is home to twenty-two federally recognized tribes, with Tucson being home to the O'odham and the Yaqui. Committed to diversity and inclusion, the University strives to build sustainable relationships with sovereign Native Nations and Indigenous communities through education offerings, partnerships, and community service.

ISBN-13: 978-0-8165-5430-0 (paperback)
ISBN-13: 978-0-8165-5431-7 (ebook)

Cover design by Leigh McDonald

Designed and typeset by Leigh McDonald in Times New Roman 11/14, Poleno, and Courier New (display)

Publication of this book is made possible in part by the proceeds of a permanent endowment created with the assistance of a Challenge Grant from the National Endowment for the Humanities, a federal agency.

Library of Congress Cataloging-in-Publication Data
Names: McCrary, Amber, author.
Title: Blue corn tongue : poems in the mouth of the desert / Amber McCrary.
Description: Tucson : University of Arizona Press, 2025. | Series: Sun tracks ; volume 97
Identifiers: LCCN 2024013922 (print) | LCCN 2024013923 (ebook) | ISBN 9780816554300 (paperback) | ISBN 9780816554317 (ebook)
Subjects: LCGFT: Poetry.
Classification: LCC PS3613.C38626 B58 2025 (print) | LCC PS3613.C38626 (ebook) | DDC 811/.6—dc23/eng/20240617
LC record available at https://lccn.loc.gov/2024013922
LC ebook record available at https://lccn.loc.gov/2024013923

Printed in the United States of America
♾ This paper meets the requirements of ANSI/NISO Z39.48-1992 (Permanence of Paper).

FOR HOSH, SHÍMA, SHÍZHÉ'É, AND SHÍNAAÍ

CONTENTS

DINÉ BIKÉYAH + COLORADO PLATEAU + PAINTED DESERT

How the garden grew 4

Blue Corn Woman 5

A relocated grief 6

Shíma and Shí 7

Brother Bacchus 9

Two Diné Men at 8 p.m. 11

To change and to be the five fingers of her 13

Manifesto for my unborn daughter 15

Book of Łeetso 17

Ł 22

O'ODHAM JEWEḌ + SONORAN DESERT

Hymn for Hosh 29

For Indigenous lovers only 33

Desert derrière 34

TC coincidence? I think not! 36

Round Dance Rain 39

Sweet, sweet Huñ (ny) 41

Natives with Neural Activity 43

Grass God 45

HA:SAÑ + HOSH + SAGUARO + THE PLACE WHERE WHITE O'ODHAM CORN GROWS

Ha:sañ 49

Self-portrait as a Saguaro 50

Weaving through a metacognition so blue, I drive six hours for you 52

Self-portrait as a Saguaro fruit 55

For Simon 56

Window Rock, AZ 58

Native girls that read Sappho write things like . . . 59

JUNIPER + GAD + WHERE THE BLUE CORN GROWS

Shí beloved 63

You bring out the Navajo in me 65

Massage my eyes, PLEASE 69

Shí Bro, Shí dá'ák'eh 77

My blue corn space is SACRED, K!? (PS protect your blue corn space girls) 80

A mixtape for a 30-something-year-old punk girl 82

3 grrrls from N. Country Part I 84

3 grrrls from N. Country Part II 86

3 grrrls from N. Country Part III 87

Blue Wound 89

Visiting the K'é in Bordertown, U.S.A. 91

Will you still see the land in me? 93

A Fighter Flowers 93

Wounded Corn Still Grows 96

This 97

Blue / corn / sky / rises above like an Asdzáá in love 98

Afterword 99
Acknowledgments 101

BLUE CORN TONGUE

DINÉ BIKÉYAH +

COLORADO PLATEAU +

PAINTED DESERT

TEA DRUNK. THIS POLKA DOT CHILD USED FEDERAL PORCELAIN TO AWAKEN THE SPINE. BE BLOOD AND CAFFEINE THIS WEEK. A GATE TO A WORD GARDEN KNEW I DON'T THINK THE STRANGERS GREW HOW THE GARDEN

Inspired by Rena Priest's "Solastalgia"

4

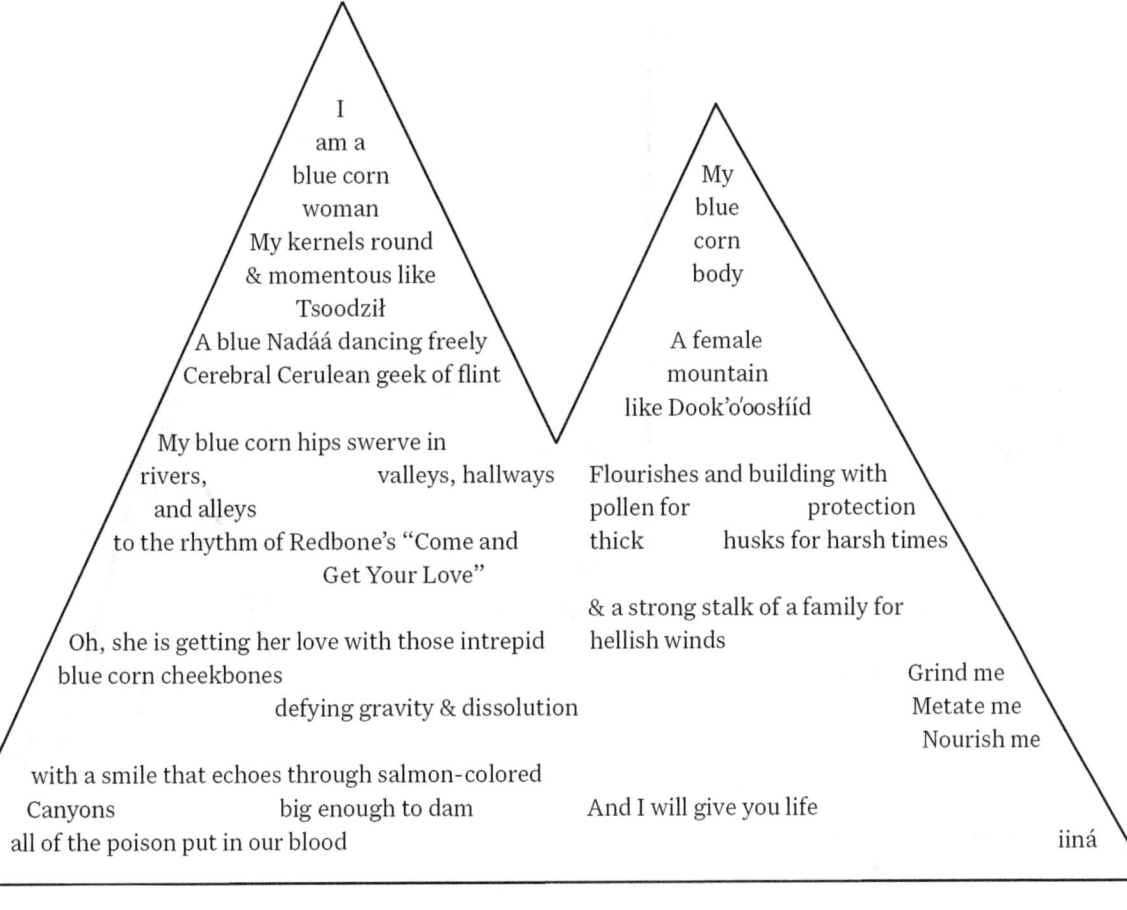

I
am a
blue corn
woman
My kernels round
& momentous like
Tsoodził
A blue Nadáá dancing freely
Cerebral Cerulean geek of flint

My blue corn hips swerve in
rivers,   valleys, hallways
and alleys
to the rhythm of Redbone's "Come and
Get Your Love"

Oh, she is getting her love with those intrepid
blue corn cheekbones
                    defying gravity & dissolution

with a smile that echoes through salmon-colored
Canyons   big enough to dam
all of the poison put in our blood

My
blue
corn
body

A female
mountain
like Dook'o'oosłííd

Flourishes and building with
pollen for   protection
thick   husks for harsh times

& a strong stalk of a family for
hellish winds

Grind me
Metate me
Nourish me

And I will give you life

iiná

A RELOCATED GRIEF

A poem about the Navajo Hopi land dispute

Father, did part of you die
the day they
      partitioned
           the   land.

    Hopi here   Navajo there

When you saw the land   leave
did part of you leave with   it?

You denounce   Diné traditions

for breviary   on hills to dry your grief

& to replace the cattle, sheep &   home taken

To replace the alcohol in   your father's blood

& the one-bedroom rock   house you grew up in

You don't like to talk about   your missing   p   a   r   t   s

then I was born and all I do is   talk about my missing parts

It's funny how_____ comes in so many forms

Will   you   take   me to the   land   where   part   of   you   died?

SHÍMA AND SHÍ*

Our eyes both like dark almonds ready to be crunched
by an older man

Roasted, ready, and reluctant
our noses grow round and hill-like,
much like a sandy hogan the older we get
the shape of our faces, unsharp but round
 greasy like frybread she makes for special dinners

Our migraines, wired for pain
weak moments cannot be *toughed out*
our worry, so ingrained it will never disappear
our hearts, curiosity spun with departing restlessness

Our clans, keeping us in line . . . circuitous nest
our nurture, she always had it
Mine came very late, along with everything else
our sadness, too common like a bloated belly

Our minds seek laughter
to flourish and fluff
the namesake of our doldrum dance

our feet stand behind bakeries and registers for years
We sit in front of fancy fruit tarts and independent movie screens
wishing for anything but small-town syndrome

Our dreams seep into one another:
castle villages, college degrees, and career language

In each meal I taste her dreams
beyond this kitchen

Frybread flying me to continents
Mutton stew showing me new languages
Spam burritos guiding me to cultures
 similar to my cheekbones

Her food, her nest
Her nest, her food, her hands
dream in my stomach

digest a strength
to go out
and
walk

many lives, paths, worlds, feasts

Shí/
    ma

* Shí: First-person singular possessive pronoun *my, mine*. Examples: shí heart, shí
squeeze, shí hunny.

BROTHER BACCHUS

Body—Brain—Fog

Brother Bacchus wakes his liver
& rips the IVs out of his skin
                    his body bogged

His anxiety controls the bottle
                    & the bottle wants to be friends
with his head

            they become best buds
they become blood

The alcohol in his blood
                    wakes
                        in
                sleazy hotels,
            cold trailers
hospital beds,
            ambulance rides,
                cop cars
                    & jail cells.

I can smell him
            his unwashed gums
        and unflossed hair
                melting in oil & plea

The blood of his K'é sees
            him walk downtown
he finds K'é with
other Diné men, they hand him a bottle of Olde English
            he drinks in a circle, camaraderie, *generosity*

The circle of Bacchanalian boys b r e a. k s
                 when
                              the first punch is thrown
         pain peels out from their skin
                              into fists balled onto faces

         Soaked nerves run dry   his libations lied

         Where is your home, brother Bacchus?

                                        Haadî Nighan Shinaaí?

TWO DINÉ MEN AT 8 P.M.

Tonight, I descend my voice
tonight, I bend my thoughts
tonight, my heart was so heavy

It should've taken
two tanks of gas
to get home

Instead, I was numb
as the tar
on the road
and dull as the red
unblinking taillights

All headed south
in lines
and in curves

I try to dismantle
a young memory
where comfort
was never an option

I continue to drive
from Plateau to
Sonoran land

with my tired mother
sleeping in the
passenger seat
toward a night sky
that holds rain
and thunder

Yet
I felt no thunder
and I saw no rain
to wash away
guilt that renders
sullen reaction
to drunken apologies
and protective pleas to stay

A brother and father
two Diné men
at 8 p.m.

one to flee from
and one to run to
tonight, I flee from both

so I do not
say goodbye

TO CHANGE AND TO BE THE FIVE FINGERS OF HER

K'é is in the constellation of my hunger
stars birth sheepherders with fast legs
and weavers with mathematical wit

K'é is the hunger of my lemniscate
tsiiyééł births the people with prayer
and prayer with infinite tongue

K'é is the lemniscate of my loyalty
where pollen births portals
of perennial hearts

K'é is the loyalty of my layers
each skin births water
and waves of Abalone Shell Woman

K'é are the layers of my haunt
each sting births a fighter
and fondness to stir the pot

K'é is the spawn of my follicle
each plot is displaced and scathed

K'é is the follicle of my forgiveness
each apology strips me frayed

and
                        changing

changing

            I am   woman

she   strokes

the whorls on my fingers

    into clay

        and I am molded

I am guided by the women of   her

MANIFESTO FOR MY UNBORN DAUGHTER

What a wonderful, wounded seed
you will be
Your Shíma
will be ambivalent about
everything in her growing life
Even you

Did you want me to say this was going to be a manifesto?
Where birth was a credence in every step
I took
For it was not

For it still is dusty in my steps
I walk through this body
of chronic maladies
and generational madness

With firm steps
And leaping chances
For the possibility of you

Forgive me for my lack of choices
And heirloom ailments

But little germ

If you never sprout
I promise I will always lay out
the finest soil
Kissed from the palms of your diné

If you, little germ, do not germinate
I will seek the finest water
to sprinkle over your little seed
And peck the pearls of your roots

For you, wounded seed,
Rest in my womb
Even if you do not come

BOOK OF ŁEETSO

Inspired by Muriel Rukeyser's Book of the Dead

THE LAND

Like graham cracker crust
milled into fine fine sweetness
Not so sweet anymore
Kinłitsosinil
Also known as Church Rock, New Mexico
Surrounded by loops of juniper, sagebrush, and blushing rocks
Population 1,128 according to the 2010 U.S. census
but you know statistics and Natives, so hóla?
63% of the people speak Diné in their homes
36% speak English in their hooghan

THE DAM

A wall
of some sort
A *protection*
 of some sort
A breach
of some sort

An open socket   oozing

Wounds wash
 and splash its blood
dry and bursting

    blood   bursts

land. crevices. waters. feet. burning feet

Burning land
Burning sand

Burning socket
Toxic sludge sits
on this open nerve

CHURCH ROCK URANIUM MILL SPILL

5:30 a.m.
United Nuclear Corporation Church Rock Uranium Mill
A twenty-foot break   bursts

uranium. thorium. radium. polonium. cadmium. iron. aluminium.
lead. magnesium. manganese. molybdenum. nickel. selenium.
sodium. sulfur. vanadium. zinc.

Spill and seep into the land

Approximately 1,100 tons
 of this radioactive seepage and
94 million gallons of heavy metal
flow 80 miles downstream
 into the Rio Puerco River

A river that gave life and water
to the livestock of the Diné

Where children played
and where Medicine men gathered
native plants and remedies
for ceremonies

6:00 a.m.
A UNC employee sees the dam breach

8:00 a.m.
A wall formation is put in the   *break*

Toxic flow into Diné Bikeyah   pauses

Residents are notified
via radio
for the English speakers only

STATEMENT

Navajos from Church Rock assert that since the accident an unusual number of calves and lambs have been born without limbs or with other severe defects.
—*New York Times*

Some people aren't going to be satisfied no matter how thoroughly you show it.
—United Nuclear (regarding allegations that the spill caused livestock deaths)

PRESENT DAY

No ongoing epidemiological
studies have been done
at Church Rock

Let's put a casino on it.

The beginning of our language doesn't begin with written word rather through tongue and sound. Tongue and sound separate me from shìnali, I could never ask her if it's true when she was a teenager, if she was excited to take the bus from Hardrock to California to learn to read? Instead, her family married her off to my nalí man. She is the only woman I have ever seen cry with her entire body, soul and heart. She smiles but I know the ocean of emotion that lies beneath her earth.

I drive home from Kinłani to O'odham land, I crack open thirty pistachio shells with my teeth. The pistachios were not open until they met my teeth. How does language open? With sound? With mouth? With vision? There are so many ways language can open and shine. I wish I could reach my nalí where my language lacks. All I can do is smile and shake her frail hand.

I am a letter that does

not fit into the

American alphabet

My mother does not fit

in the English

Alphabet

She fits

in the spaces between

the letters

unseen and caring.

My dad does not dream

in the Anglo Alphabet

He dreams

for the safety of his

drunk son and rigid

daughter

One at home

and the other in

another state.

Somewhere between 70

and 45 degrees

A bolt strikes through

L

Descending diagonally

from the right

A bolt, unlike an arrow

A falling discord

A line of beauty given

to us from the eastern

sky

Ł, isolates myself from a
band of USA-ians
I sit in my office, I try to
teach a co-worker how to
pronounce Kinłichiinii
A word and clan passed
down maternally for eons of
seasons
I sit patiently, make eye
contact
Clasp my tongue to the hard
palette of my mouth
And make a noise, air flows
constricting much like a
hiss
After the fifth try,
co-worker gives up
I return to my sandy desert
& Nali does not speak
English
I hear a vibrant array of
glottalic consonants,
nasalized "aa's" and
accentuated syllables
When she talks to my father
"Yá'át'ééh shiyáázh, Áá'
ha'íí baa naniná?"

Now she is still there, her Ł's
and áá's and íí's will always be
on point
like her Diné rugs
94 and still weaving
like the badass Asdzáán she is

                    Matriarchy rules
everything around me

I have this little L with a
squiggle through it,
Ł breaks down the walls of this
colonial maze
It guides me around bits and
pieces of a
kin kind of tongue
I carry Ł with me everywhere I
go
Under my tongue
Sometimes it hibernates in my
cheek
beneath my lower lip
Or in my belly after a morning
of blue corn mush
An untaught letter
I grab this letter from the
eastern sky
And place it my mouth

Ł

The truest form to who I am does not exist in the American
alphabet
The truest form to who I am can never hold a conversation
with my nali

O'ODHAM JEWEḌ +

SONORAN DESERT

HYMN FOR HOSH

I.

I walk down to the sinuous Sonoran
Full of sinful thoughts
and a sublime soul

A pond of oil glistens in the sun
sits like melted butter on Alkąąn crust
after a day of monsoon musings
water on sand sends goosebumps through the land

On hills and valleys
Covered in phallic philosophies
firing out your throat

In the pearl of morning
The heat spins me naked
I search for your rain house

II.

noise nectars an intrinsic ripple
desert honey pulsates

                              sticking to the sky

Spreading a frequency

III.

//When he listens closely//

//an electric orchestra buzzes fruitfully//

I wonder if he hears my own
ballad buzz
with each poem painted
on my tongue

My song is heard
& my ancestors sing

They can't help but take notice

They tap a toe
drum a finger or two
with a half-smile
splashed across their face

the scale of my chorus heightens
when my Diné cheeks redden like a prickly pear, sliced into halves
sweet and unstrained

my hum is heard
when I'm
in solitude, washing dishes, in my apartment
thoughts only
smiling down with soapy silverware and
sponge in hand
scrubbing, rinsing, repeating

My hums crash into one another
like porcelain on steel

When I drive home after work on the 10
the sinuous saxophone solos vibrate on the freeway's overpass
& Sade sings to the sun

this sleepy star drifts behind Muhaḍagĭ Do'ag, South Mountain

musings hover above, a lilac amber horizon
into honey lavender clouds, they shift

The sweetness of the sky flashes in and out of the clouds

Ember strokes lift and light up the horizon

    Oh, sonorous Sonoran!

        hues sinuate through the electric horizon
        my follicle aches

        & I swallow the nectar of its sunset

        with each golden drop, I am released

IV.

In the hollow hums of circular silence

I hear his fluttering smile
greet me from across the room
his lips plump into the blush of cactus flowers
when he stands next to me
the red beet in my chest wants to collapse
into itself like a fussy sinkhole

In the baritone of his body's chorus
I hear the tenderness in his silences
and awakened flesh in ripe syllables

Hibiscus hues embarrass my smile
& stream into my belly
My belly is flushed for the desert's sweet honey

His golden knowledge sparks and sticks to me
like bursts of spit in a fit of laughter

Something grows
and something lets go
calm and continuous
like a wave

A tune begins again &
our song swells until
the levees our fervors break,
soaked into parched pastorals

The sands of our skin melt into each other
like roasted velvet mesquite created by the hands & stones
of his people, desert folk,
my Ha:sañ
        Shíhosh

In the sensuous sand
his spine stands strong
playing song after song

        with each hearty hum
                the nectar of our throats sweetens the scrapes of our sorrows

FOR INDIGENOUS LOVERS ONLY

He dashes upon each deck
and tells me my cheekbones hold up the sky

I, in solitude, go back to my penumbra of a room
He, flies back to the Sonora, returning to his cactus cave

I return to my nestle finding scattered coins sleeping on my floor
His black socks sweeten the ground for company

weekend desires exist like seasons
time is an illusion

pants are pulled off, skin is bared
coins unknowingly slip from fabric to floor

If money is imagination of the glutton
we are skin and bones

We suck at succulent broth of the other
on top, the tips of my cocoa-colored hair tickles
his smile lines and sweep across his browbone

I move my hips like mountains
wide and heightened
until location must be changed
location must be remembered

Place is a memory
and we are nomads
exploring and reliving this land
season by season, skin by skin

I turn my cheekbones to the sky
and hold them up for you

DESERT DERRIÈRE

Its fluffy billowiness like baby cheeks
is the derrière of my homesickness
the pit of stiffness

Its glazed homemade dinner roll derrière
dawns on the horizon of my slapping hand

Rather a massaging like hand
not a finger or nail
to display light strawberry streaks across skin

For my desert derrière
must always have gusts
have an uncreased sand dune

Each grain falls into place
creates a perfect butt of a hill

I do not want to shovel or mark it with pity
but with rain from my tongue to skin

Do not mistake my diligence for
unfulfilled lust
but filled wildness

Filled savagery like a Twinkie
sticky, sweet, and unapologetic

But give me some credit
this little indigenous gal
likes to havoc a little hell

No dairy air ever comes out of this Divine derrière
rather noises in the bathroom
that it thinks I do not hear

So I laugh in the bedroom
because it's my happiest moments not known
even to the desert derrière of my desire

I have to say from time to time it sets me on fire

TC COINCIDENCE? I THINK NOT!

Twenty years and some change later
we meet and learn
we both lived in the same
Rez trailer park

you know the one behind McDonalds
by the trading post
on Moenave St.

We laugh about it
because when you're poor
sitting in sadness is too easy
too dilapidating
we aren't easy people
humor gives us another day to live for
jokes, only trailer park Rez kids understand

Your Tuba City slang
surprises me
and I cackle
in bed, museums, bookstores, cafes, the car
in metropolitans, suburbs, and little Rez towns

twenty-plus years later, we meet
twenty-plus years later, we are sweet
with one another

On the couch
you try to speak Navajo
with wide eyes
you grab my hips and say in your low voice
Shi heart, Shi Girl
I scream Stop!
I laugh so hard my cheeks might explode

if it weren't for my round hazelnut skin
keeping them intact

You continue to repeat romantic Rez words
 and look into my eyes
my stomach is full of luxury
my brown belly wants to fart with laughter
but I yell Stop!
because I would be too embarrassed
 if my body reacted as such
the Rez kid in me has learned her limits

I move and sit on the floor of my living room
and browse through an early 90s edition
of *Native People's Magazine*

A Michael Chiago painting animates the glossy page
I hold up the magazine
 and show the painting to you
it is of an O'odham village

Men and women are holding hands
they are in a circle sidestepping with each beat
The Sonoran Desert in the background
purple mountains blend into the mango horizon
you say, *it looks nice*
 smile and continue reading for your grad-school class

I look closer at the picture of the men in the painting
Mr. Chiago is spot on

I say, *you could be one of the men in this, they look like you*
you smirk because you think I'm making fun of you
but I am not
your low soft sleepy O'odham eyes
with broom-like eyelashes straight and thick
always manage to sweep me away

your olive black shoulder-length hair and horizontal mouth
look like the T.O. grandpas round dancing in the painting

I like to think of an old you, cheii you
your hands the color of theirs
hickory with darker hints at the knuckles and elbows

I close the magazine
and lie on the couch next to you
I want to interrupt you so bad
and play like rowdy Rez kids in the boonies

but we are now Indigenous grownups
living in the city
heirlooms of our nation,
Diné and O'odham
reading and living toward a better future
from what our mothers and fathers had

Alas, I get up and take a shower
so I do not disturb you

ROUND DANCE RAIN

The muse of my desert
the dessert of my muse

I want to eat all the sands of your desert sweetness

Give me every grain in the whole Sonoran
I will crunch and swallow every bit
take the sweetness of the desert
place split saguaro fruit into my palms
and I will place it on the ground face up

Its sweetness returns to the sky
then back to my lips
and I will swing and stomp in a million circles for you

Our round dance brings the sweetest rain
it enters a circle
much like the sun
but within my throat I feel it
swirl into a million soft cacti
piercing each part of this sadness
and yearning
700 miles away

Take the spikes and put them in a bag
so they will retrieve my morose thoughts
and hang them on a wall for me to call art

for me to make a zine
for me to make a pie
for me to make a lie

A cactus frame
of your face in the middle
because in the forest of my dreams

I lay in it
and I'm living in it

SWEET, SWEET HUÑ(NY)

In a sea of bitter calloused kernels
swimming in their own douses
of germination

You are the softest, sweetest, and genial
despite the error of excrement
you were given

wayward weeds abundant
& infestations undeserved

Quite contrary, you did not run elbows with concrete
or vicious winds

You took your seed, soil, and soul
and made
    midnight sky silk

My eyes beat seashells
for your sixty-day kin
you gift me season after season
thousands of years of yourself
how do I live up to the return
I wonder?

            I look at you
          sober as a corn
         silk corn hairs
            tied back
        frays sticking out
              whole
           & unhulled

Gliding along Pima canals
from West End to East End

I look at you
sober as a maze
man of a maize

NATIVES WITH NEURAL ACTIVITY

The silent subtleties of
natives with neural activity

around these relatives
boom to the ears of the corn
blast to the beans temples
and cuddle the cotyledons

seeds with technology and instinct
KNOW

they swoon into the soil
caress and cradle

roots spread
and stir
with dirt in between
swollen bulbs

the weight of a
tender energy
guides down and deep
for they know it's time
to germinate
by the time the sun's
heat hits the west

To gift
to nourish
and to continue a cycle
of some kind

perspiring preparation
laughing anticipation
leads to a new season
and hope

The water is ready
and
the sun has not come
soon enough

Oh loins of desert sun!

I wait in my village/
for no one/but here
you are/my
cloud
of summer/

my maize god
of prickly pollen
paths/

Seize me!

You cousin of grass/wit of luck   /container of kernel/

obsessor of history/ sex of stalk

Raise your corn silk / let it down/be my companion plant

I wilt for no one/   except for your leaves to hold

Shade me on the driest of days/   and I will keep your home unpaved

from unrelenting teeth/ sorrow's secretion hollows your home

hair of saguaro seeds/my moon desert solstice   Backbone of my tongue!

Rainhouse of my heart!

swim in the glitter sand-waves

HA:SAÑ +

HOSH +

SAGUARO +

THE PLACE WHERE WHITE

O'ODHAM CORN GROWS

HA : SAÑ

The soft mesquite of his spine
wears the day so well

My juniper skin
craves the fuchsia light

The silhouette of my trunk
engages in your pleats

A pleasure, a pop of colors rotates
I ignore all the colors behind your head

Your hair twirls slightly inward
with the southern sky

Saguaro seeds blend
 into your eye's pupil

Adorn with age, fruitful

Melting into the magenta
of my thighs

SELF-PORTRAIT AS A SAGUARO

Sometimes I feel like you
    a flowering hosh, has:an, saguaro
    breathing in the rocky sand

A bright boiling star
    eyes my waxy, sprinkled skin
    I look at you and I can feel the prickled
    toothpicks stand on my skin
    just like when I see
    the hosh of my eye

I feel like you before the monsoons
    my ribs dry from the heat
    ready for the rain
    & the new year

However, this year is particularly funny
but not so, what does this tall saguaro know?
    the rain is solemn
    the rain does not repeat
    like it used to

I see relatives pick off
    my bearable fruit
    for years longer
    than something called a nation state
    whatever that is

Sometimes I see you leading
    me to hosh older
    than the state of Arizona
    standing taller than the
    politicians looking like over-watered prickly pear
    with pricks spilling out of their mouths
    poking and bleeding out
    letters with no song

Sometimes I feel like you
    seeing freeways being built
    over my relatives and friends
    feeling the rivers dry in my spine

My belly unfull
    in the heat
    the magnificent heat
    under my weight
    I am protected beyond the laws
    by something stronger
    something laws cannot govern

When I see you
    my belly is full
    & the rain clouds appear
    bustling, dripping, rested

Please let it keep raining
My spine crackles
in between love and loss
of language and land
the cars spit grief
in the name of sacramental songs

A terror to us, a barrier between my skin and song
We can't hear it anymore
only the sound of wheels
whizzing and whirring

all in the name of construct of the mind
the loveless of the sands

it is raw in your belly
it is raw in their language
it is raw in a bleeding mind

Please do not let my belly disappear

WEAVING THROUGH A METACOGNITION SO BLUE, I DRIVE SIX HOURS FOR YOU

Our blue corn thoughts weave
through the loom of my musings
you are the male strings
holding my female strings together

Place your palms on
my loom's creation
fiber hairs stick out
teasing your nose
with a tickle

My hands hold stories
in this weaving fork

the holy people bring colors made with
tea, yucca & juniper berries
to paint the color of our world

Desert smiles
wind me down
from my densely packed walls

I have to leave once more
Please do not forget me
in this golden state ha:san

I will send you poems, watercolors,
 and pictures of this sleepy water land

Your yucca strings reel me in
I spin with delight and stupidity

a path formulates from the Sonoran Desert to the redwood forest
to bring you my love

Midway and six hours
My waxy war pony
spins on black pavement
spits and spurts in love
on the I-5 between Oakland and LA

Between the violets and greens
of my mind's wool
my sad chiddy weaves through countless cars
speeding past me along this central Californian road

I surrender to this oscillating ocean
my water bleeds to the desert

steering wheels selvedge steadily
one driving north, the other south
under a blue corn sky
until our thoughts touch

Love is not merely for the privileged
if there is one thing us destitute
are well-crafted in
it is the craft of love

a rebirth of love, land, language
Gháájí' to Bahidaj—we dance to celebrate,
the fruit of our thoughts never static
this indigo maize shines like a gaze from ghastly eyes

Somewhere between violet and green is me
somewhere between violet and green is you
everything else is light and darkness
sleeping and waking in the earth's sky

corn kernels grind on our tongue and minds
dehull the husks of my desire
take the tassels and rub them into
marigold pollen

SELF-PORTRAIT AS A SAGUARO FRUIT

Slice me open like a saguaro fruit
    let me bleed, raw red with delight and comfort
    take your carob thumbs and rub the skin soaked

My needles fall out easily for you
    unlike the others, I've made sure to stab in all the right places
    so they can let me be—to bask in the sun

I was not ripe until
    you knew the clouds would be here soon
I was not ripe until
    you knew the rain would cleanse my spirit
I was not ripe until
    you saw the brightness in my stamen

Thank you for letting me bask
 as long as I wanted

Then you can enjoy
 the crimson of my fruit

FOR SIMON

Some say it was a crow
some say it was a red-tailed hawk
flying above the brown hollow

I didn't know he liked to fish, I say
Neither did I, he says

We sit and eat; a projection of pictures rotates on the screen
friends, family, students
eat this meal for you

I have never been to this part of Arizona—Mohave Chemehuevi territory

We trade driving positions at Quartzsite
I comment about the mountains, *It's like a painting*
you don't say anything

I wake up at 5 a.m.
lightly scratch your back with my right hand
I'm going to get up and shower, I say
your body is enervated, on its side and turned toward the wall

I shower, dress, and make tea
I return to the room
It's almost 6 a.m.
you slowly rise

I can feel the weight of the germs in your chest
my eyes lower to yours looking puffy and historic this morning
We need to leave soon, I say

The importance of our morning is two and half hours away
This sets in motion and you lift from the bed
and into the shower

I check emails on the couch, after I am done
I go to the bed to find you dressed
collapsed vertically on the mattress
your bare feet hang limp

I grab your hands to lift you up upright

It is time to bury your best friend

WINDOW ROCK, AZ

Today I
saw   two
native   lovers

sharing   a   tamale

at the Saturday

morning   flea   market

It made me think of you   285 miles south of me
So I save   a blue corn cookie

with piñon nuts   for you
I laugh and hope   I don't bring it back

c r u m b l e d

If it gets   to you

unbroken

Then

I
will   smile

NATIVE GIRLS THAT READ SAPPHO
WRITE THINGS LIKE . . .

Give me a chance to miss you
your heart warm like   apple pie
and silences   light as the crust of said pie

Awkward beginnings call for midnight sex
          and dances not yet formed

 Until we dance together
     bind our steps the way our bodies
  move   between rooms or noises
Unlearning your intimacy

          is like forgetting my clans

        or where I was born

JUNIPER +

GAD +

WHERE THE BLUE CORN GROWS

SHÍ BELOVED

Shí beloved moves
with caution into a
forest of billowy bark
this new-found Plateau intrigues him
as he sidesteps, wispy with thirst, fruition, and vigilance.
Juniper's twisted branches arouse
him, his palms cup the curves and bends
of the silver splintered bark
cloudy lines curl into its cortex creating tangles
for his eyes only like a fine-tooth comb
he detangles what he can and falls to his knees.

Shí beloved gulps
the asdzáá air around him
puffed mesas sink into cinnamon sand
& popping junipers
dance upon the rounded peaks.

Shí beloved spreads
his fingers wider than the mesa
 he stands on and savors the orange desert pulp
with each breath in. Juniper's branches spread
wildly and whistle in the untamed wind

shí beloved's ears rise
with curious blood

Shí beloved dreams
with tension, uncertain
with the sensation serenading in his gut
falsettos grip his throat in pollenating bursts
Shí beloved does not understand this stamen tucked under his tongue
indigo berries flood his mind night after night,
juniper ash fills his bones and
flurries his mind with each sheepish step

Shí beloved anticipates
alone with these knots in his thoughts
on his own tangled path, his steps curl into circles
This silver arch of Juniper
is dancing to be seen and
these berries are waiting to be squeezed

Shí beloved climbs
countless mesas for this whimsy tree
till his convictions rub his soles into bone
stepping tiredly on the salmon-colored rocks

Until his eyes see the trunk of the whirled wood
peeking out of a coral canyon wall,
juniper does not scream to be fixed,
rather adored for its odd foundation

His prudence beams into the color of wild lavender
azure clouds levitate and dissipate into the winds transport

Shí beloved's thoughts
rush like water into the fine sand

Shí beloved dances
with the trees
taking him further from anything he's ever known
like a tree without bark

YOU BRING OUT THE NAVAJO IN ME

After Sandra Cisneros's "You bring out the Mexican in me"

You bring out the Navajo in me
sand waves bursting out of my skull

You bring out the fighter in me
jalapeños in your guac
ghost peppers sending a punch through your salsa
red cinnamon-lace nights in me

You bring out the dancing flame in me
mountains of candles
melting like a sucker in the sun
slurping your heated heart

My tongue cannot wipe clean what it does not know

You bring out the love weight in me
bellies bumping in the shower

you bring out the
commod bod in me
the hardened leftover lard
from frybread feasts in me
can't sleep naked in bed anymore

You bring out the Diné in me
conquered tongues and colonized lips
washboard Rez roads along my spine

You bring out the fool in me
hibiscus grin teeth
stained from my ruby woo lipstick

Nevertheless! My love is not naive
I am also the hell-raiser
the blasting glare
The mean, thin-lipped, cosmic cheek stare
fighting for the next day
next pay
or way
through road blocks and never-ending rejections

I am the child mourning over mountains too tall for my dreams
I am the woman burdened and bare
I am the gash gouging through skin, bursting to care for your seeds
I am the fool tricked and naked searching the night's sky for light

A fool to lover
your throat takes me through tunnels of
gasps grounding me into deep, deep sublimity
surrounding me with saguaros, salt, and spikes for these wounds
It digs deep until my throat scratches into the brightest blood

Dear shiheart! Oh, how you
bring out the lover of life in me
drunk on George Strait love songs in me
dancing until my feet pop

You bring out the poverty in me
fighting for scraps
without judgment in me

You bring out the hidden trauma in me
the condemned bulldozed boarding school dorms in me
the Spanish kidnapper in me
the exploiter in me
the broken treaties in me
the big words we don't understand in me
the stories the sea cannot wash away
the slippery shame we try to escape
from street to street with our legs and our bottles

You bring out the days of sickness in me
Stiff back, congested lungs
& tight sinuses in me
endless chronic suffering, spinning me through loops of pain

oh! does my love suffer, shi heart, shi hosh shi lover!

You bring out the blue corn in me
leaving sapphire flour all over your kitchen counters
between your teeth and underneath your fingernails
the blue does not stain but grits against your tongue

You bring out the yellow corn in me
I tap my tassels for you
sift polished pollen
for your tádídíín bag

You bring out the strength in me
body builder in me
Rez gym in me
bi's and tri's days in me
the after-workout protein shake in me

You bring out the saní in me
making sure you're fed
crying if you're misled
the shíma that outlives all her sons
the always there in me

You bring out the generations in me

the sheep herder
the weaver
the changing woman

       the First woman

             the Spider woman

                                                              in me

You are the one I make bread for
brew Ch'il ahwééh for
Pick out manly-smelling candles for
learn about all your favorite 80s wrestlers for

let into my little home
lay my head on your lap for the first time
hold your hand until my stomach leaps oceans for

The one I blink my eyes for
to know, this is not a dream
                                        &

                                                    if it were to be a dream

                                        your sky soars with abalone clouds

sopped with the
rain of your love tongue

                                        onto my shell

MASSAGE MY EYES, PLEASE

After Fatima Asghar's "Ways I Am Tired"

How many times has someone uprooted my radicle before meeting me?

My lover bleeds out asdzáá with a digging stick
to my spine, slices the kernels off
they fall on asphalt so hot
It can cook an egg
or pop a corn

All my life I tried to forget who I am
and live like a bright clean canvas
unstoried but well kept

I've sat in Chiang Mai train stations
and waited for love
in Nepali cafes
tucked in Thamel corners
with white men
just as confused as me

Train after train
A green leaf leaves
too fast for me to hold its palm

My millimeter of root
shuffles in the air like the fine hair
of my arms and scalp whorls

A man sits across from me
salivating with scissors in his hand

he wants to clip my tiny root
to forever hold in his palm

One day he will cash it in
to a museum or antiques roadshow

he will act like this pretty little root
flew into his hands
even tho conquer
 is carved into his eyeballs

he will buy a mansion with this pretty little root
but will lose it in a few years

because he didn't keep up on his property taxes

I read about a native poet
who keeps their place of origin a secret
and I don't know who to trust anymore

I read about femicide suicide in El Salvador,
mass shootings in chain stores,
and women with my face missing
all over turtle island

And I type—
the only way to protect my little root
with radical expression

The only way to guide my genocidal grief
without migraines, nausea, or stolen breath
painting their pain in my body

Last weekend my lover and I went
out to the First Friday art walk
at the local native museum
They had a boarding school exhibit

we maized through the rooms
familiar as grandma's tortillas
on a Saturday morning

As we walk out the exhibit
a white woman tells her white date
My ancestors didn't come to the states until the 40s
they were not part of that!

/Part/
/of /
//THAT//

If I had a cup of tea for every white person
compromising their own part of American
history that doesn't involve genocide or racism
all their excuses in the world would
give me my own ocean of tea called
The Bay of White Supremacy with a hint of fragility honey
oops I mean The White Nationalist Harbor for a Free America
with a hint of Patriotic Honey

Somewhere a white lady tells her date
she never had no part in that
but yet here we are
in this nightmare

I turn on the TV to see an orange snake
slither its tongue. and its scales fly back revealing
its blue blood
I keep thinking it's a dream
it will go back into the dank hole it came from
It doesn't matter what year it is—
there are still concentration camps
on our soil
there is still blood at the borders and occupied lands

I think of the babies, the mothers' feet
heat and deserts—
thirst

then in sixty years a bilagáana woman will say
my ancestors were never part of "THAT"

I drink my lavender tea
and turn off the lights
it is not a dream
I shut my eyes as hard as I can
and I am still tired

SHÍ BRO, SHÍ DÁ'ÁK'ÉH

When he drinks
he replays a five-year-old me
& eight-year-old him

walking one morning
from our Tuba City trailer park
to the boarding school

I cross the road too soon
A car speeds and plunges
into my five-year-old frame

I don't know how you lived!
You were rolling around under the car and you went into the tire, do you
    remember!?

Memory only recalls waking up
on the ground without
a scratch
And a man with a dirty car and a dopamine
tongue yelling a million miles per minute

I went to school that day and forgot all about it—

When he drinks
He tells the story over and over
About the little boy in him that was scared
of his little sister that didn't listen
and crossed the road

I still don't have a strong memory
Sometimes trauma is strong like a can of HG

When he drinks
he says, *if we stick together, we will be ok*
I think of myself three hours south
in a dry desert with a lush life
Compared to what I used to have up north
a bleeding juniper, berry-less, fruitless sinking into the earth

Diné love is a funny love
It can be cruel and enlightening all in one gasp
Diné family is circuitous love
Full of passivity,
we didn't know we were supposed to be listening
for something

Last week, brother was in a coma,
ICU from his DTs
seizures in the brain

My mother and father visit him every day
even though he can't talk
even though he is sleeping
even though he has stolen from them for just one sip
even when he keeps us up late into the night until cops are called
even when he gets kicked out of rehab and a search happens because he is too
    drunk to realize where he is
even when he lets strangers into our home, and they steal
even when he talks about death as a desire
even when quitting sounds like a luxury

They say the desert we come from is barren
How little do they know about the land.

When he drinks
I think of the safety the three-hour distance has
My lesions remain botched
Cuts are cauterized

I wait for the seasons
And cook savory soups with my saguaro

When he's sober
We go back to saying nothing to each other
And laugh at nothing

Unenlightened by our seasons gone by

MY BLUE CORN SPACE IS SACRED, K!? (PS PROTECT YOUR BLUE CORN SPACE GIRLS)

Dedicated to all the fuckbois of the world

You are a bright white period
that does not know how to end a sentence
an eggplant scab of a zit to be scraped off
but resurfaces
& delves deeper into a desperate root
like a bright pink bubble gum
in the armpit of my ears
uproot this lie
you are still clinging onto

Waters settle until another storm destroys the ground
 Why are you here?!

Who asked you to come?!
you are the malignant hand
twisting my roots armful by armful

Under the moonlight I sleep
with silk and dance
with pollen
you are the shovel
uprooting my blue corn dreams
my blue corn growth
tossing aside for what?!

your power is as sick
as the bile you sleep in

in the dewy earth
my vulnerable soil
you thirst for
and grab in one fistful
hungrily scrap and toss
this isn't a ride or rollercoaster
but an uprooting of my salvation

My being, my stalk, my kernels
were shining in the moonlight
And dancing in the pearly plateau wind
Why are you here?

Why do you still cling to this dirt?

A MIXTAPE FOR A 30-SOMETHING-YEAR-OLD PUNK GIRL

Give me the 30-year-old punk
With experience
Give me the 30-year-old punk of color
Unafraid of the skinny white boy
Testing my 1970s record collection
The slits were more punk
Than the sex pistols
Founded by a now-ridiculous Johnny Rotten
And racist-ass Sid Vicious

Give me the Diné girl giggling
In the alley all in black
Reclaiming her sexuality
At every turn

Give me the 30-year-old
Navajo punk still listening
To her X records, skipping
From all the scratches
Letting the blood pulse in this body of anger

Give me the shy Navajo goth girl
Unaware of her worth
Her driving that used to scare the shit out of me
Her kindness louder than Al Jourgensen's smashing screams

Give me the loud Navajo girl
Quick to punch, slow to flower
Our red blood molds us in these alleys

White and red
Such a strange concoction of violence
Sparkling with unending nerves

Leather on leather
Black jeans crusted with holes
Dead Kennedys patches, slaps of dead hair dedicated to Danzig
Sponged with iridescent valours

Kick this 40 oz into gear
And throw me into the swirl of
stinky white and brown bodies
Let me be confused by my anger
Let me be confused by the racism
Let me be confused by the sexism
Let me be confused by dreams of escaping all that I know

Give me this body I have now
That understands it was a dream to be confused in my own curiosity
With a kickass mixtape
Letting my brain shrink in all the alcohol, drugs & romance of dead

Give me this 30-year-old body living
Give me this 30-year-old punk lady
Still dreaming of the world beyond that alley in that small town
Give me all that is forgotten
Give me what I hoped to forget
And let's celebrate

3 GRRRLS FROM N. COUNTRY PART I

after Bob Dylan's "Girl from the North Country"

If you're travelin to North Country dread
Where the winds hit heavy on the Red

I wonder if they remember me at all
many times, I've often thought

In the dawn of my morning
In the sleepy sun of my eye

It all becomes clichéd memoir
and scribbled journal entries

A doused liver dances in midnight mixes
Eyes swell
into a sweaty toe of a hindrance

Glory, guts, and punk
three Diné girls
singing the anti-american dream

into Mother Mountain's lighting ear
she hears our spirits
in this back-country sky

Our torpid spirits teeth bottle caps
& laugh into violent liquid

Death is at every corner
but we don't know it
so we listen to music about it

Silent woes
hide in the sands of internal suffocation
Gives way to choked seeds

How silly to be an age of any kind

Mind mumps
Viral thoughts of the past—

If you're travelin to North Country dread
Where the winds hit heavy on the Red

If you go when the snowflakes fall
When the sky deepens, and the tender ice is tall
Please see for me, they are wearing a coat so warm
To keep them from the deathly wind

I wonder if they remember me at all
many times, I've often thought

Remember me
for they were once true loves of mine

3 GRRRLS FROM N. COUNTRY PART II

Cultivated   Clouds
            Crimson   Lips

Twist   Smear   over

                                    drunken   anxiety

Lightning   love   busts

                                    battles   blindly
                              ////

                              Fever hunger   tears

                              black   eyes

                              Leather   casts bodies
                                                  back & forth

                              Tell me

Tell   //   them

                                          before vomit

passes my lips//

                        they hold my arms
                                  and
                              love me

/Tell me not to miss this/

3 GRRRLS FROM N. COUNTRY PART III

Some of us wanted to die
some of us didn't think we were worthy
of a single kiss, a hand to hold

Some of us were ready to tear our pants off
in the glory of the anti-american dream

Either way, we all wanted love
in those dirty, puke-covered coves

A brown girl to woman
even if she is far before her years

Our cheeks hold up these sacred mountains
even if we are misfits
crying to clouds, to release us
from this small-town hell

Release us from this little well of wishing

Release us from this school
where three girls from the North Country
would meet next to my locker
next Mr. Blackgoat's Navajo classroom
where we failed our tongues

Release me from this memory
of how life was Nizhónígo Iiná
with Three Girls from the North Country

Release me from this life
of mourn
of Three Girls from the North Country

Release me from knowing
our wild ways

Tell me not to miss this.

BLUE WOUND

Cerulean slashes, I walk away from—
an infection to ignore for decades
a tear from the earth
a tear from the spirit

Gardens gash gently out
skin and spirit tear violently in
farms funnel through fire and bone

Transparent spirits flood down reckless throats
bleeding into infected alleys
this concrete was not made for us to grow

gutter water is not warrant of these wondering welts
seeds sprout through wounds, *unsaved* lands & fields

Grains germinate in gashes
CRASHING not skywards but upwards
BREAKING through the land
the sun kisses a cicatrix cosmo

But some seeds would rather hide in the womb of our earth
than be born into a blue wound

When really, I'm the wounded sky
You put your arm under my neck when we sleep
The bone of your lower arm cranks my neck into stone

I see you as a reflection of pain and poetry
When really you see yourself as routine and wonder
It is your delight to see the storms roll in on time every year
My wonder is where do these storms come from? What makes them dark?

I play the cheery teeth for all
When you speed past folks without having to sell your soul
Your wound falls short on others
Maybe I romanticize it because I am a poet, a wound, a *non-muse*

Do I romanticize too much of what is not there?

VISITING THE K'É IN BORDERTOWN, U.S.A.

Its hue took me by the hip

Where the lack of—

        suddenly became

An abundance of—

The lack of me   cracked between an abalone ajéí and bleeding daze

Pushed out—

The lack of me, phased out, in this country

I was silly and sequestered where it started

         I loved the forlorn
         for it was all I knew

These streets, rarely lit, take me by the hip
Tell me to grieve the lack of me

In a town,
In my town
In my parents' town
In my brother's town

In a town
That bewilders us into their wild tongues

         they slither sardonically
         we close our eyes
         like feared children

walking without sight
without lights
through these streets

The lack of me
Once blinded—

sees the brightest blues

WILL YOU STILL SEE THE LAND IN ME?

You are ~~not~~ divine
Boarding school made
but burning

Your mind
filled with forgiveness

Your tongue
glows when you speak to your mother

A burning beauty
thunder-spark burdens
your western consciousness
into concrete

As a child, you were ~~not~~ divine
sheepherder feet of the tangle people

abandoned thrice by mother, father, and maybe god
I can't tell if it is forgiveness, denial, or a short-term memory
that breathes life into you everyday

What awe, to believe a story I try to tell
but only bleed

Blood is laughing
our throats boil
to recognize sorts
when all is scattered

Tender will you be as an old man

will you still see the land in me?

A HUMBLE BREEZE WAFTS & WATERS THE DAY THEY ALL TALK IN SEASONS STEAM FLOATS ABOVE SLEEPING SEEDS

A FIGHTER FLOWERS A FIGHTER FLOWERS A FIGHTER FLOWERS A FIGHTER FLOWERS A FIGHTER FLOWERS A FIGHTER FLOWERS A FIGHTER FLOWERS A FIGHTER FLOWERS A FIGHTER FLOWERS

ajéí ajéí ajéí ajéí ajéí ajéí ajéí ajéí ajéí ajéí ajéí ajéí ajéí ajéí K'é ajéí ajéí ajéí ajéí ajéí ajéí ajéí ajéí ajéí ajéí ajéí ajéí ajéí ajéí

FLOWER FIGHTER FLOWER FIGHTER FLOWER FIGHTER FLOWER FIGHTER FLOWER FIGHTER FLOWER FIGHTER FLOWER FIGHTER

A HUMBLE BREEZE WAFTS ABOVE SLEEPING SEEDS

STEAM FLOATS THEY ALL TALK IN SEASONS & WATERS THE DAY

ajéí ajéí ajéí ajéí ajéí ajéí ajéí ajéí ajéí ajéí ajéí ajéí ajéí ajéí ajéí ajéí ajéí ajéí ajéí ajéí ajéí ajéí ajéí ajéí

K'é

ajéí ajéí ajéí ajéí ajéí ajéí ajéí

WOUNDED CORN STILL GROWS

Weaving words with nostalgic tongues, heirloom futures, and circular knowledge.

Praxis to the Mind. Hózhó. Himdag.

Contact and exchange of Diné Blue Corn and O'odham White Corn.

Nourish the soul. Huñ. Naadą́ą́

Planting O'odham melon and sending photos of the Sonoran

                         January, female rain.

Bring me back

to you. Niséyá

THIS

This is ~~not~~ a song
This is ~~not~~ a chant

This is a breath

        a ~~moment~~

A story

              a telling of plants

Growing under a sun
Growing with the dirt they were given

It is a telling of companion plants finding nutrient in one another
Creating a soil rich for their seeds

For the next season
For the next harvest

A place to breathe
A place to shine
A place to home

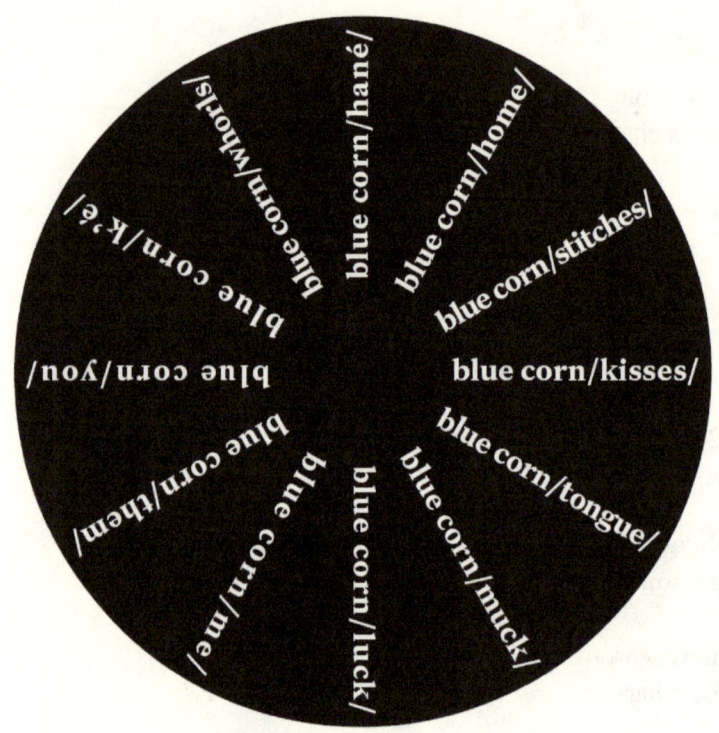

The extension of my body is blue corn rising from the canyons of Sháá'tóhí
The extension of my body is blue corn rising from the canyons of Sháá'tóhí
The extension of my body is blue corn rising from the canyons of Sháá'tóhí
The extension of my body is blue corn rising from the canyons of Sháá'tóhí
The extension of my body is blue corn rising from the canyons of Sháá'tóhí
The extension of my body is blue corn rising from the canyons of Sháá'tóhí
The extension of my body is blue corn rising from the canyons of Sháá'tóhí
The extension of my body is blue corn rising from the canyons of Sháá'tóhí
The extension of my body is blue corn rising from the canyons of Sháá'tóhí
The extension of my body is blue corn rising from the canyons of Sháá'tóhí
The extension of my body is blue corn rising from the canyons of Sháá'tóhí
The extension of my body is blue corn rising from the canyons of Sháá'tóhí

AFTERWORD

THIS COLLECTION started when I was teaching kids on the Salt River Reservation about the importance of eating their fruits and vegetables. I did not expect to fall for one of the teachers. I was simply a low-wage worker who was secretly writing poems at work the first three hours of my shift then spending my afternoons talking with folks in Salt River about plants and food sovereignty. I did not expect to be experiencing intimate moments and dreaming of planting O'odham corn, tepary beans, and squash in the Sonoran Desert, but sometimes life can feel like a weird rom-com. As Chawa Magaña from Palabras Bookstore called the first two years of my muse's and my friendship (yes, it took two years for us to gather the courage to state our feelings for one another), it was a "saga."

Falling in love as a Native person is funny; so much is involved with intergenerational trauma, and there is enough baggage to fill a dump truck. I hope Natives can see my love (as a Diné woman) for this person and for their O'odham culture, land, and plants. In return, they showed the same. Sometimes, I joke they like my culture, land, and plants a little too much, i.e. cheekbones, juniper trees, and Tuba City.

I had no intention of writing with the language of my mother tongue (Diné) or my muse's language (O'odham).

I was born in the Tuba City hospital in 1987 and lived for a short time in Shonto and Black Mesa before our family moved to Flagstaff. I never intended to be a writer. I was not the type of child that told her peers that she wanted to be a writer when she grew up. I thought that was only for rich people, people that lived in big cities or children whose parents were lawyers and professors. In the eyes of a girl from the Rez and a small town, it seemed that the only voices that people listened to were white or wealthy. I was neither.

As a teen, I was a quiet punk girl living in a reservation border town in Arizona. Little did I know that my parents were only able to acquire a home because of my father's family's involvement in the Navajo-Hopi land dispute. At a young age, my father always talked about how the dispute and relocation of their family changed his life; land grief and loss spilled out of his mouth many evenings. I didn't understand what he was talking about because I was going through my own obstacles: racism, sexism, colorism, classism, chronic illness, and a deep depression. I felt so much shame and didn't understand why. Once I left that small border town in Northern Arizona, my whole world seemed to open up, and I began to find the answers I was looking for. I took American Indian studies classes at Arizona State University and felt like pieces of a jigsaw puzzle were coming together before my eyes. I finally understood why waiters were so rude when my family sat down at a restaurant and why Peabody Coal perpetrated land violence on Dinè Bikèyah.

After I got out of my small town, I backpacked around parts of Asia, where I realized other travelers were very interested in who I was and what I had to say. I was very happy to tell them all about myself. I would save train tickets and receipts to museums and collage them; I'd write letters to 16-year-old me about how life would get better.

Some of the poems in this book talk about self before land memory, blood memory, and self-love. Some of these poems talk about self after the learning to love myself and the land as a Diné woman.

As Jake Skeets writes in *Nihikéyah: Navajo Homeland*, "It is through language that we can further sculpt the idea of homeland. Land as form is a constraint that is beyond Western poetic forms and is employed by Diné poets because of the way land informs form and not the way Western constructions inform language."

So, with my hope and memory, this is a story of a girl who remembered the land. I am a woman that does not come from a culture nurtured by Western society; therefore, some of these poems are crafted and written in a way that is not centered on Western techniques of craft or creativity.

I'm a girl that has remembered the land and I am protecting what I remember through language on these pages.

ACKNOWLEDGMENTS

THANKS TO my family—Mom, Dad, Delray; my Shonto family; the Dan family (and all the Dan girls); Charlene Dan and Fred Johnson; Grandma Cowboy; my Nalí Faye Begay Furcap; my Hardrock family; Sarah Clark; Stephen Kensley and family; the Nez family (Jean, Sandy, and everyone).

Thank you to our animals living and passed on: Pacino McCrary, Sandy McCrary, Ponyo McCrary, and Charlie McCrary. You have no idea how much you have healed us with your love and loyalty.

Thank you to my friends and colleagues who believed in me when I didn't believe in myself: Becki Coleman, Chawa Magaña, Denise Dominguez, Jeff Slim, Kinsale Drake, Chanti Jung, Sierra Edd, Julie Fiveash, Anne Clay, Shaina Nez, Ryan Greene, Tatè Walker, Chelsea Hicks, Byron Aspaas, Manny Loley, Charissa Lucille, Jake Skeets, Casandra Lopez, Esther Belin, Laura Da', Laura Tohe, Tyler Mitchell, and Tanaya Winder. Thank you to my Mills MFA family: Rai Rai, Mimi, Erica Lee, Matthew Wong, David, Claire, Arya, Marissa, Oliver, Darius, Joanna, Booz, Truong, Stephanie, Elmaz, and Julianna. Thanks as well to my Indigenous Nations Poets family, the Palabras Bookstore family, Julianne and Brenda from AZ Humanities, the kind folks at Native Arts and Cultures Foundation, the Projecting All Voices fellowship program, and Tolsun Books.

Thanks to the zine community. If it weren't for y'all, I would have never realized I could write or that people cared about what I had to say.

And thank you to the land; without you, I am nothing.

Some poems from this book originally appeared in the following publications:

Poetry: "Blue / corn / sky rises above like an Asdzáá in love," "Blue Corn
   Woman"
Room Magazine: "A relocated grief"
Yellow Medicine Review: "Manifesto for my unborn daughter," "Shíma and
   Shí," "Window Rock, AZ"
Bluestockings Magazine: "Two Diné Men at 8 p.m."
F*%k IF I KNOW/ BOOKS: "To change and to be the five fingers of her"
Santa Fe Literary Review: "Sweet, sweet Huñ (ny)"
Mayday Magazine: "Grass God"
National Resources Defense Council: "Self-portrait as a Saguaro"
Hayden's Ferry Review: "Hymn for Hosh," "ShíBeloved"
Blacklist Me Zine: Honoring the Poetics of Native American Music: "3 grrls
   from North Country," part I
Electric Deserts: "A Mixtape for a 30-something-year-old-punk girl," "Desert
   Derriére," "Round Dance Rain," "TC coincidence? I think not!"
D.A.N.G! vol. 3: "3 grrrls from N. Country," parts I, II and III

ABOUT THE AUTHOR

Amber McCrary is a Diné poet, zinester, feminist, and artist raised in Flagstaff, Arizona. She is Red House clan born for Mexican people clan. Her paternal side is from Hardrock, Arizona, and her maternal side is from Shonto, Arizona.

She is the creator of the zines *D.A.N.G!* (Daydreaming Awkward Native Girl) volumes 1, 2, and 3, *Angsty Asdzáá: Tales of an angry Indigenous woman*, and *The Asdzáá Beat*. Her chapbook, *Electric Deserts!*, was published by Tolsun Books. McCrary is the owner and founder of Abalone Mountain Press, which is dedicated to publishing Indigenous voices. She is a board member of the Northern Arizona Book Festival, was the recipient of the 2022 AZ Humanities Rising Star award, and is a Native Arts and Cultures Foundation LIFT awardee.

You can find her poems, interviews, and art at *Yellow Medicine Review*, *POETRY*, *Room*, *Poets and Writers*, and *Hayden's Ferry Review*.

She divides her time between Northern and Southern Arizona.

For more information on McCrary, go to www.ambermccrary.com.